Before You Begin Advertising

A Workbook for Small Businesses

Cheryl Berry

Copyright © 2018 Cheryl Berry

All rights reserved.

ISBN:1984392395
ISBN-13:9781984392398

TABLE OF CONTENTS

     Introduction

1. Assessment
2. Why Advertise
3. Before you Advertise
4. Digital Presence
5. Cost of Customer Acquisition
6. Distributing your Budget
7. Effective Advertising Schedules
8. Types of Media
9. Understanding Measurement
10. Final Reminders

INTRODUCTION

I am going to take you back to whence I began my journey in the Media Industry. In 1994 I was fortunate enough to intern for The New York Times Co and The New York Times Magazine Group. At the time, NYT Magazine Group was a powerhouse owning more than 12 popular magazine franchises

I worked and learned in several departments over 4 years, Research, Promotions, Event Marketing and Advertising Sales Teams. I was privy to "special projects" and research being conducted. Two large focuses at the time were (1) What the demographics of the United States would look like in 20 years...or hmmm right now; and (2) What to do with this thing called the Internet. There was one small shared department between NYT and NYT Magazine Group where they studied and contemplated the vastness of the possibilities. In just four years (the 12+ titles magazine tiles were reduced to 4 the rest being sold off. It was foresight that "Print" was beginning its decline. Less than 3 years after that, The New York Times Company sold off the remainder of its magazine group. Today, quite a few of those magazine titles are completely extinct not even surviving their new ownership.

Fast forward the last 15 years I have worked in Broadcast Television Media. The last 10 years I have truly witnessed the shift in media consumption. With the Introductions of new technologies, the rise of social media, streaming stations. The consumer has 15x more choices for entertainment than they did 20 years ago.

With so many more choices, a predicament has faced Advertisers, "How to best advertise and Penetrate to Customers?" I have seen large National clients and advertising agencies stumble through it. The content within this book is meant to assist a small business or a business new to advertising get on the right path from the beginning in a workbook style.

ASSESSMENT

What are you doing right now?
Write down all of the ways you are advertising right now. Include the free forms of advertising as well as the paid ways. Include sponsorships of any kind. Networking events, fliers, door to door. Do not forget the small donations to local school teams, coupon books, churches etc.

Why are you doing it?
For everything that you are doing, write down the reasons for doing it. Do you see anything you don't have a good reason for?

Who do you reach?
Who is your most likely client. Who is your ideal client. Who are you currently reaching as a customer. Is this similar or different from your ideal customer?

What do people currently know about your business and the service or products you offer? For example they know your location. They know you offering Heating and Air.

What do you want them to know? Do they know your service area.

Would you like them to know you offer warranties.

Is there something people have a misconception on? Do you get people thinking you do something you don't do? What do you want people to know prior to them contacting you?

What is your avg profit? Sale price of product- cost of product- advertising or overhead expenses

What is your close ratio? For every person that comes into your business or calls you, how many do you sell to?

CHERYL BERRY

What are you doing right now?

Why are you doing it?

Who do you reach?

Who do you need to reach?

What do they know about you?

What do you want them to know?

What is your average profit?

2 WHY ADVERTISE?

There are several reasons why people advertise. To determine the type of advertising you should engage in however, you have to ask yourself many questions and drill it down to the most finite of reasons.

Example:

Have people somehow forgotten about you and you now need to Create Awareness? Do people already know you but now you are introducing a new product or service? Are you trying to make people aware of a new location? Are you trying to attract more of a particular clientele? Are you having a sale? Are you currently spending $100 for every new customer you acquire and you would like to reduce that cost to $50? Is your current client base drying up and you are looking to reach a new client base? Are you trying to improve your reputation or express that your business is under New Management? Whatever the reason remember that the underlining goal of Advertising is it is an investment to keep your business stable or to assist your business in growing.

Traditional purpose of advertising– To reach as many people as you can as many times as you can for the least amount of money possible.

Refined purpose of advertising - To reach as many of the "right" customer as you can as many times as you can for the least amount of money possible."

Digital/Online Purpose of advertising – To reach as many customers as you can at the right time and at the right place while they are looking to buy.

We just covered the general purpose of advertising. Now let's get into the specifics of your business. Why do you want to advertise? Ask yourself the following questions:

Is my business trying to?

Create Awareness

Provide Solutions to Customer's Needs/Problems

Generate Leads and/or Traffic

Increase Sales

Lower the cost of customer acquisition
Improve Profitability

You may not have an answer for every area above. However, with any item your answer should be and you should take the mindset of that your advertising and marketing is **an Investment.** If you can't see a clear path on how what you are spending on advertising will provide you a return on investment then ask yourself, "Should I be doing this?" "Does this make sense?" If it doesn't make money, then most likely it does not make sense. Eliminate it from your marketing plan.

3 BEFORE YOU ADVERTISE

What type of business are you? Are you a destination spot? A luxury item? Will people travel 20-50 miles to come to you or you to them? Are you the type of business that people will typically stay within their general vicinity, 5 miles from home or work.

A destination business will need greater reach for survival. A convenience based business may just be wasting money by reaching out too broadly. Define your Target Audience.

Do not be ashamed to state who your customer is. I have had Pastors of churches tell me they want to reach people who have the income to "tithe". Be realistic. Will people really drive to your location? Is your business easy to find?

Who is your most likely customer? I hear to frequently that a business's customers are women. However if I stand in a grocery store for hours, I may see an equitable amount of men and women. Perhaps a woman is your best customer. Maybe she spends more overall. However, she isn't your only customer.

Therefore again be realistic. Have you taken time to understand who is currently doing business with you. What do they look like? How old are they? Where do they work? What is their ethnicity? Their income range? Who are your best current customers?

Look at all of the customers currently doing business with you and now decide who is your best customer. In addition to who spends the most with you, include who is a repeat customer. Who provides referrals. Who is the least amount of headache.

Start Tracking your customers:

If you aren't currently doing it, start quietly surveying your customers. Count how many people walk into your doors daily. Check and see what time people are calling you. Be careful and again don't make quick assumptions. Be creative. For example: If your business provides service to vehicles. Don't assume the type of music your customer listens to, check the radio station their car is one when they bring it in. In my experience most customers cannot correctly identify what media source they spend the most time with so ask them more general questions such as their favorite programs or the types of things they enjoy.

What type of business are you?
_____

Define your Target Audience.
_____

Who is your prospective customer?
_____

Who are your best current customers?
_____

Who spends the most money with you right now?
_____

Identify:
Geography _____
Age range _____
Gender _____
Ethnicity _____
Income _____
Lifestyle _____

If this information changes based on the type of product or service you are offering, then complete this worksheet for

BEFORE YOU BEGIN ADVERTISING

each different item.

Before you advertise, review your sales patterns. I am surprised at the number of businesses I meet with that do not Review their Sales Patterns.

Information such as when do you conduct most of your business. Drill it down. What are your best months, weeks, best days of the week and your best hours. Match up your sales patterns to your products. Match up your sales patterns and align them with any particular customer group.

Example Family Diner: Slow month December. Busy month July. Slow on Monday and Tuesdays. Selling more Takeout on Fridays. Perhaps a large amount of Single people during the week. More families on the weekends.

What are your best selling or most profitable items or services? Is your business doing really well with a particular product but it's your least profitable. Do you need more focus elsewhere?

If you don't have the answers to these questions or enough data from your own business then examine the sales patterns of your competitors. Sometimes this information is published. If the information isn't published consider looking through organic information online.

Organic information as opposed to "paid" search information is a good indication of when customers are naturally in the market to buy something versus being pushed or led to a business.

Good resources include: SPYFU, Google Analytics. Department of Labor and Bureau Statistics.

Review your Sales Patterns:
When do you conduct most of your business?
- Best month _____
- Best weeks _____
- Best days of the week _____
- Best hours _____

What are your best selling or most profitable items or services?_____

4 DIGITAL PRESENCE

I have done almost identical campaigns for similar types of businesses. If 4 out of 5 campaigns are successful I have gone back to review why 1 was not successful. A commonality has been 4 of the businesses had a polished online presence. The one unsuccessful Businesses did not. Imagine a Real Estate agent with no website. Imagine a Service provider such as a roofer or plumber with bad reviews.

Remember the way people consume media today is much different. Suppose someone sees your Television advertisement or hears your radio advertisement. Today's consumer is savvy. They will immediately, or make a mental note to later research your business or check you out online. They will not only look for your products and services but they will also look for your reviews.

In some sense a business that advertised in the past on Television or Radio gained automatic credibility. "That business must be good because they are on TV." This is still true to some extent, but it can be derailed quickly with a large number of bad reviews.

If you have no reviews, consider giving customers and incentive to leave you one. 10% off their next purchase.

Monitor your reviews. If someone leaves you negative feedback, do not let it go unaddressed. Take the conversation off line.

Tips: Make sure your branding and logos are consistent across all media forms.

Remember a "good story" can go viral, a "bad story" will go even further.

How is your digital presence? Rate yourself on the

BEFORE YOU BEGIN ADVERTISING

following areas. Do you have all of these things active and in place? Do they look consistent?
   Website_____
   Social Media_____
   Google directory_____
   Reviews/YELP etc_____

Are you actively monitoring these things? If you have a contact form ensure that the email account it links to is consistently monitored. A great campaign can be derailed if leads from that campaign are not worked proficiently.

5 COST OF CUSTOMER ACQUISITION

Before you advertise determine the industry standard for your type of business to invest in advertising. A proper business plan budgets 3%, 5%, 10-15%, even upwards to 30% of Sales. Try to be as specific as possible to your business line. Within the legal profession Person Injury Attorney's on average invest more than other legal specialties.

I would not expect a business with an average profit of $10 to spend the same amount as a business with an average profit of $1000. Unless, the business with the average profit of $10 had multiple locations and the business with an average profit of $1000 had a singular location. I would advise in any scenario, to not spend anything at all if you cannot budget for an adequate or purposeful campaign.

Now when evaluating advertising options determine:
- How many leads and subsequently sales would offset the investment of the advertising. If you are paying for leads, place a value on leads from each media source. You may find that leads from one source are more valuable and spend more than leads from another source within the same medium.
- Develop metrics for Traffic, Website, Calls, Leads, New Customers, Sales. Is every new customer a repeating customer or a one-time purchase. If a repeating customer, multiply.
- Dollars invested in Advertising divided by New Customers
- Dollars invested in Advertising relative to Sales growth
- Deduct cost of product or service, Dollars invested in Advertising from total sales price.
- COUPONING: Do not coupon unless you have built it

and the cost associated into your advertising strategy. Beware of couponing too frequently. Customers may only purchase your product or service when they can locate a coupon.

- Determine the industry standard to invest in Advertising – 3%, 5%, 10-15%, even 20% of Sales

- How many leads and subsequently sales do offset the investment

- Develop metrics for Traffic, Website, Calls, Leads, New Customers, Sales

- Dollars invested in Advertising divided by New Customers

- Dollars invested in Advertising relative to Sales growth

Many businesses do not think they have an advertising budget. However when they add up all of the minor sponsorships a small business owner may quickly realize they have spent a sizeable amount that could have been invested into a structured campaign with an effective media source. However, without proper planning a it just hasn't been structured.

6 DISTRIBUTING YOUR BUDGET

In the previous section, Cost of Consumer Acquisition we discussed determining the overall advertising budget based on your businesses industry standard.

Now that you have your overall budget you must determine how to distribute your budget across the vast array of media forms.

For your particular client base you may already know what forms of media are more effective. In some scenarios you may have to test various mediums to see how they perform.

You will need to use the information you have about your best consumer and match it with nationally known consumption habits of that consumer base.

For example: Let's assume your business sells "hearing aids". Your best customer is 60+. Analyze media consumption habits of people 60+. If you see that they spend 3 hours a day reading. 6 hours a day watching TV and 1 hour a day online, Your budget should be distributed accordingly. 30% to Print Media, 60% to Television and 10% to Online Media.

Now let's assume your business is a training school. Your ideal customer is 18-34. You may be hard pressed finding your customer reading the newspaper. Instead your media consumption habits might look like 6 hours on Social Media. 4 Hours Watching Television. Your budget would therefore change to allocate 60% across online platforms and 40%

across Television platforms.

Do you see how the medium form you choose changes based on the product you are selling and the demographic you are trying to reach?

On the next page there is a chart from Statista. One of many companies that analyzes and provides data on Media consumption. It is noteworthy mention that this data changes regularly based on Day, Month, Quarter, Season. Be sure to look for the most updated Data. Take a look at the chart and see how media consumption can change drastically across a selected demographic.

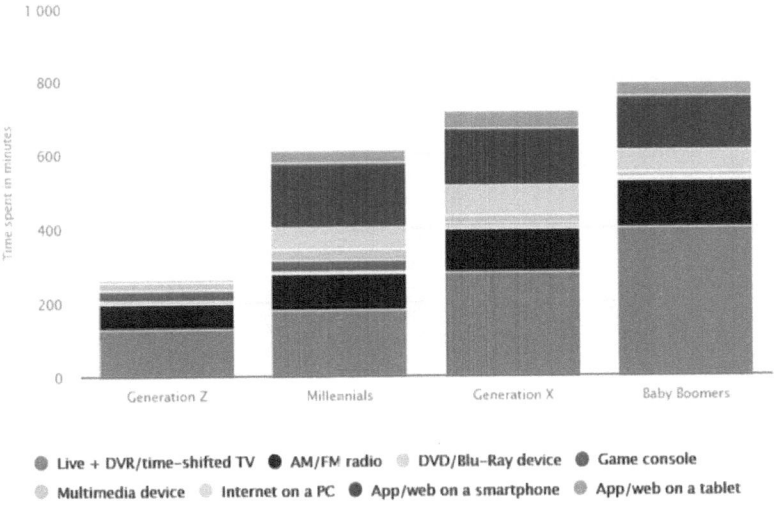

What do you notice on this above chart about media consumption? Do you see the Baby Boomer age group spends almost zero time consuming media on game consoles. Generation Z does spend time viewing media on game consoles but almost zero time with media on Internet, Apps on web or smartphones or Tablets.

There are several other ways media consumption data can be viewed. It is common to find reports by gender and race as well. The above chart is from Stastica. Other companies I recommend that provide similar information are Pew, TVB and Emarketer. Try to choose an independent source for research.

7 EFFECTIVE ADVERTISING SCHEDULES

A successful campaign utilizes two major components. The science of schedule and placement and effective creative messaging.

The science of the schedule is bit different from traditional media forms and digital. Here is the basic theory for traditional media such as Television, Radio and Print that is commonly used by a small business. The science of the schedule is commonly referred to as "Frequency and Reach".

<u>Frequency</u>

BEFORE YOU BEGIN ADVERTISING

The more times an ad is seen (heard) the more people respond to it.

Research previously showed that an ad must be seen 3 times to achieve an actionable threshold. Now research states action at 8+x due to media inundation

<u>Reach</u>

The cumulative effect of how many people an ad reaches.

Target the optimal reach & frequency based on the desired results

In a world where people are exposed to numerous advertising messages a day frequency is used to "cut through the clutter". It will take time from the time a person first sees a message, to acknowledgement and recognition to taking action.

Reach is how many people will be exposed to your ad. Your business wants a good balance of reach and frequency. I would want my small business to be exposed to 50,000 potential consumers 10x as opposed to 500,000 potential consumers 1x.

consumption habits of people 60+. If you see that they spend 3 hours a day reading. 6 hours a day watching TV and 1 hour a day online, Your budget should be distributed accordingly. 30% to Print Media, 60% to Television and 10% to Online Media.

Now let's assume your business is a training school. Your ideal customer is 18-34. You may be hard pressed finding your customer reading the newspaper. Instead your media consumption habits might look like 6 hours on Social Media. 4 Hours Watching Television. Your budget would therefore change to allocate 60% across online platforms and 40% across Television platforms.

Do you see how the medium form you choose changes based on the product you are selling and the demographic you are trying to reach?

The sort of creative your most likely customer will likely respond to.
- What type of emotion to place in an ad. Differentiate.
- The type of language that should be used Inform.

- The sort of look and feel that would most appeal to your client Differentiate.
- Whether or not you should include instructions in your ad. Educate.
- Whether or not you want to direct your client to call you, visit you in person or go to your website. Create Action.

Make sure that your "branding" is consistent across all medium forms. If a client sees one font and logo in one place and another in another place it will dilute the strength of your brand. Consumers may get confused on whether or not you are the same company.

Beware of using online images. Make sure the image you are choosing isn't watermarked.

Check Up: Does your business name. logo and slogan make sense for the type of business you are in and the type of customers you are pursuing. Could your messaging be offensive or alienate any particular segment of your consumer base.

8 TYPES OF MEDIA

Now that you know who your business is and what your goals are as well you have determined more about your customer and your desired customers we can examine different mediums in more depth. Based on your goals and your customers and where you can find your best customer you are ready to look at the various mediums and their attributes.

Review the geographic footprint & coverage of the medium you are considering. Does it meet your businesses purpose. What are the demographics that the medium form reaches. What is the reach and frequency potential of the medium. What is the customer responsiveness typically. Is the medium form Intrusive or Passive. What is the CPM or vCPM of the medium.

Intrusive

Television/Cable
Radio
Pre-Roll Video/Display Ads
Outdoor

Passive

Newspaper
Magazine
Direct Mail
Internet/Websites

Intrusive media forms may influence a customer that they need something. Will impede upon a customer when they are not shopping and create desire. Ex: TV makes you want a hamburger

Passive medium appears quietly and customers who are already shopping or seeking something are likely to happen across passive medium forms on their own. Ex: Online you already know you want a hamburger and are trying to find the best reviews, coupon or closest place.

9 UNDERSTANDING MEASURMENT

When you receive a proposal for placing media you may come across terms that you aren't familiar with. In my experience in the sale of advertising customers will make reference to certain media jargon without full comprehension of how it is applicable to them and their business.

For instance- here is a question Radio and Television hears often from clients. "What are your ratings like?" As a professional I frequently follow up with, "Do you know what a rating is?"

A Ratings point (RTG) equals 1% of the population being referred to.

For example: If you live in an area with 800,000 Homes then 1 Household (HH) Rtg = 8,000 Households.

In the same area 1 rating can also be applied to a specific demographic. If there are 2 million people within the age range of 18+ then 1 rating point or 1% of this demographic would be 20,000 people 18+.

If you in scenario of Households are in a program with a 5 rating, then you would be reaching 40,000 Households. If you are in a program with the scenario of a 5 rating in People 18+ you would be reaching 100,000 people.

In a media scenario we assume that 1% and sometimes even ½ of 1% of people reached will be drawn to your business after hearing or seeing your ad.

Ask yourself now, could your business adequately handle the flow from 1% of 20,000 people or 200 customers? 1% of 100,000 people or 1,000 people?

I prefer to speak to small business owners and recommend that small business owners use Cost Per Thousand when reviewing measurements.

Although media forms are NOT apples to apples this is the closest way to put them in similar terms when analyzing media across all forms.

What aren't all media forms comparable when providing measurement numbers?

In Television or Radio when provided a reach number, that is the actual estimated number of people expected to view or see your advertisement.

In Print the circulation number is the number of homes, or places an advertisement is delivered to. There is no guarantee that the mailer is opened or that the page your advertisement is on is read. However, print circulation also has a 'pass along' rate. In addition to the place the print piece was delivered to, it may have been passed along up to three times.

Cable and Satellite or ADS-

Remember Cable and Satellite TV are not the same as Broadcast TV. In a given marketplace Broadcast TV reaches 100% of a market. Cable and Satellite reach those homes that "pay" for service. There may be multiple Cable providers in a market. Make sure you get the Reach numbers for your cable system not the entire market. This will provide you with better accuracy.

vCPM- Viewable Cost Per Thousand is a relatively new term when referring to Reach online. Just because your advertisement is on a media site, it doesn't mean it is always in a position to be seen. To place in comparable terms with other media, you need to use vCPM not just CPM.

Here is a general idea of what you are looking at for CPM across media forms:

Direct Mail

A typical CPM for direct mail is **$26-$27**. However, that cost can vary greatly. When calculating the costs in the equation, it's important to include all costs for producing and sending direct mail. These costs include graphic design, mailing list rental, printing, mail house fees for addressing and inserting mail pieces, and postage. Marketers can lower the CPM by finding ways to save on any one of these steps in the direct mail process.

Magazine

CPM for magazine ads is calculated on the estimated circulation size of the magazine, which you can find in the magazine's media kit. Most provide audited figures, including the total number of readers broken down by subscribers and newsstand sales. Using the total circulation estimate provided in the media kit is an acceptable calculation method. The average CPM for magazine advertising is **$8 to $20.**

Billboards

Billboard advertising offers advertisers the opportunity to reach the estimated 70 percent of people who drive to and from work each day. Stationary billboards advertise everything from local hospitals to fast food chains. The CPM for billboard advertising is low, ranging from **$3 to $5** nationwide, but offers little opportunity for tracking and measuring effectiveness. It is also difficult to estimate with any certitude the number of motorists that pass and read billboard advertisements.

Keywords

Keyword advertising displays concise text ads and links to

advertiser's websites during Internet searches. The ads are chosen based upon keywords and phrases that people type into search engines. Advertisers "bid" on keywords like an auction, setting maximum thresholds for their bids in advance. Keyword advertising CPM varies based upon the words chosen. The average range for keyword ad CPM is **$5 to $20. vCPM used as alternative.**

Social Media

Social media marketing is a relatively new marketing tactic. Marketers often track both the CPM and the CPI, or cost per interaction, for social media, and they use both metrics to judge the costs and effectiveness of their marketing efforts. The average CPM for social media banner advertising is **$1 to $4**. CPI or CPC is **$7-$22.**

HULU/INSTAGRAM- Streaming Service **$30-40 CPM**

10 FINAL REMINDERS

Remember if you don't know your reasoning for advertising in a certain way then you need to re-evaluate your plan. If a particular sponsorship or media does not fit into your goals you have defined you need to quit. Put aside a proper budget for your advertising. Before you assume you do not have a budget look around and add up every penny of spending. Fliers, business cards, coupons, school sponsorships can add up quickly. If you can only afford 1 form of media but not 3 then start with the 1 form of media.

You must know your business and your customers to create a campaign and a strategy that will impact your business.

- Know your business
- Know your customer and their behaviors
- Do the math.
- Evaluate and measure
- Don't dilute yourself.
- Know why you are doing something.
- If it's not making you money, it's not making sense.
- Set up a system to Evaluate and Measure
- Consistency and Persistence

- It's an Investment

www.ingramcontent.com/pod-product-compliance
Lightning Source LLC
Chambersburg PA
CBHW030032250526
45464CB00025B/1369